# I AM WITHIN

## ROSEANNE D'ERASMO SCRIPT

This book is dedicated to the memory of my mother, Mary Agnes Hurley, whose life and passing spiraled me into a search for meaning early in my journey of life.

AuthorHouse™
1663 Liberty Drive
Bloomington, IN 47403
www.authorhouse.com
Phone: 1-800-839-8640

© 2012 Roseanne D'Erasmo Script. All Rights Reserved.

No part of this book may be reproduced, stored in a retrieval system, or transmitted by any means without the written permission of the author.

Published by AuthorHouse 10/09/2012

ISBN: 978-1-4772-7372-2 (sc)

Library of Congress Control Number: 2012917759

*Any people depicted in stock imagery provided by Thinkstock are models, and such images are being used for illustrative purposes only. Certain stock imagery © Thinkstock.*

*This book is printed on acid-free paper.*

*Because of the dynamic nature of the Internet, any web addresses or links contained in this book may have changed since publication and may no longer be valid. The views expressed in this work are solely those of the author and do not necessarily reflect the views of the publisher, and the publisher hereby disclaims any responsibility for them.*

## References

Chopra, D. (2003) The Spontaneous Fulfillment of Desire, NY, NY: Harmony Books, Random House, Inc.

Chopra, D. (1991) Creating Health, NY, NY: Houghton Mifflin

Mentgen, J. & Bulbrook, M.J. (1993) Healing Touch Level 1 Notebook, Carrboro, NC: North Carolina Center for Healing Touch

Millman, D. (1995) The Laws of the Spirit, Tiburon, Ca: H.J Kramer, Inc.

Rathbun, R. (1994) The Way is Within, NY, NY: Penguin, Putnam, Inc.

Williamson, M. (2004) A Gift of Change, NY, NY: Harper Collins, Inc.

Zinn, J. (1994) Wherever You Go, There You Are, NY, NY Hyperion

*T*he day is quiet, as Marissa, Joey and their teacher sit on their favorite bench in the garden. They are surrounded by the colors of summer. The trees provide a cool green canopy over them as they gaze at the beautiful garden of flowers.

"Teacher, the garden is a rainbow today!" exclaimed Marissa.

"Yes child, the garden surrounds us with peace as we learn to be calm and go within."

"Go within? Where are we going?" asked Joey.

"It is within our inner selves. Some say we are centering. We are able to feel energy around us."

"Sounds different. I am not sure I understand, Teacher," said Joey.

"It helps us pay attention in a special way, being focused on right now, the present moment. We just let our mind and body be still."

"I sure have busy days. The only time I think I am still is when I am sleeping," said Marissa.

"Yes, we are all very busy but one of the keys that is needed to have a happy life is meditation, which is the stillness we are discussing. It is your guiding light to help you see the way."

"Wow, if meditation can bring us a happy life, why doesn't everybody just do it?" asked Joey.

"Excellent question, dear one. It is because meditation is a discipline of the mind and body and it feels uncomfortable for most people. It is a universal connection and a place of miracles."

"Miracles, I like the sound of that! Tell us more, Teacher," said Marissa.

"It is a way of stopping, letting the goop around us thin."

"There's goop in me?" asked Joey.

"Well, it's more like a cloud around each of us, and we have to clear it in order to go within to look at the spirit inside," explained the teacher.

"A spirit inside…a ghost?" asked Marissa.

"No, no, my child. It is about YOUR spirit within, YOUR energetic self, YOUR being."

"Hmm…," pondered Joey.

"Sometimes the best way to learn is to simply do the work. I do believe that now is the time to begin our exercises."

"First, we must be comfortable. Use a chair or pillow, put your feet on the ground, or sit cross-legged, and concentrate on being right here, right now."

"Okay, I will go on the bench across from Joey. I am comfortable," said Marissa.

"Me too," agreed Joey.

"Next, start breathing, observing the flow…out and in, without controlling it, just observing."

"Teacher, I am thinking about things, like baseball and a sub sandwich!" exclaimed Joey.

"That is normal. It is what happens as you begin. Just keep your awareness on your breathing. Be fully present to this moment, this time, this breath."

"What is awareness, Teacher?" inquired Marissa.

"Child, it means to concentrate on what you feel, see and hear. Just let go of your thoughts and breathe."

"Okay, I am breathing. I think I get that part," said Marissa.

"Concentrate on your breath, in…out…in…out," said Teacher.

"But it feels funny… to not be doing anything," said Joey.

"Ah, how observant you are. It is just because you are not used to it. Non-doing does not mean the same as doing nothing. The joy of non-doing is that nothing else has to happen right now."

"So I just enjoy sitting around being me?" asked Marissa.

"Yes, you are seeing this time as perfect. You have no agenda except to be fully present. Nothing else has to happen."

"It still sounds hard, Teacher," said Joey. "I don't get it."

"All right. Let me help you. It is the following of one breath to the next."

"Well, THAT sounds easier," said Joey.

"We can be at home wherever we find ourselves, at peace with how things are, by breathing in the moment."

"That makes more sense. I feel that way in a baseball uniform-then I'm ready for baseball," shared Joey.

"Now that's an interesting thought. But you don't need a uniform-it's simply YOU, your inner self, your inner being!" said Teacher.

So the teacher, Marissa and Joey sat for a while, breathing, relaxing and letting the moments flow. They followed the outflow and inflow of breath.

"It is like seeing something from behind a waterfall. We still see it, but we are not in the foam," explained the teacher.

"So we don't get soaked, right?" commented Marissa.

"Perfect, Marissa, we don't get rushed by the water of thought or feel stressed about our day."

"I heard Mom and Dad talking about stress and we even talked about it at school when we were going to be tested," said Joey.

"Yes, meditation and becoming centered can help relieve stress. Are you comfortable?"

"Yes Teacher, and I am closing my eyes and focusing on breathing in and out; in and out," said Joey.

"Okay, now slowly watch your breath in your mind. You may add a saying like ho-hum, or ah-ha. You may start louder and then let both breath and sound get softer. When you quiet your breath, you quiet your mind."

"Okay, Teacher. It is very quiet. I hear my breath, but I hear birds, the wind and the trees too," said Marissa.

"That is all right, little one. Keep your mind open for just this moment, just this breath."

"It is still hard not to let my mind wander," said Marissa.

"Practice is one of the keys to feeling comfortable with meditation. We have to take each moment as it comes and let it flow. It is important to be patient," explained Teacher.

"Are there different ways to focus?" asked Joey. "Suppose I wanted to have a picture in my mind to help me. Is that okay?"

"There are many ways to focus, child. Some people use images of mountains or ideas like love, kindness, hope and patience. Once you learn to focus on your breath, you may move into these reflective meditations."

"Teacher, if meditation is so important in our lives, I still don't understand why we all don't just do it?" wondered Joey.

"Child, somewhere in our path, our own thinking mind gets in the way. We talk ourselves out of trying something new and different."

"So we have be open to listening?" inquired Joey.

"Exactly, my child," said Teacher. "Now, let's try another image. With your feet on the ground, breathe in and out. Concentrate only on your breath. Picture a grassy hill with a beautiful tree in the middle. You are walking up to the tree and feel at home having a seat on the rich, lush grass. In front of you is a pond that is calm… still. A pink lotus flower blooms on a lily pad. You look up and see the sunbeams pouring through the clouds. It feels so peaceful. The pond can hold anything that you put into it and it can bring you images or insight as you look upon it."

"Okay, Teacher, this is fun," whispered Joey.

"But is that it?" asked Marissa. "Just sit and breathe and look into the pond?"

"Not quite. Now invite yourself to breathe in and out and look up at the sky. Sit down by the tree, quietly breathing, allowing whatever it is you need to come to you. We look at our own lives and become very still with wisdom. We breathe, in and out, connecting with the strength of the tree."

Teacher, Marissa and Joey sit quietly together. They are practicing. After a while, Teacher says, "Children, it is time to ask yourselves what you have learned from the tree and the pond. Take three deep breaths to center and ground yourselves."

"Teacher, I feel very quiet, yet I have a feeling that I can do anything!" said Joey.

"And I feel very sure of myself!" exclaimed Marissa.

"And that is what you need for the moment, for now, for today. Each experience will be different for you. Each experience will be different from the next time based on your own inner need, wisdom and layers of angst."

"Angst?" asked Marissa.

"Yes, feelings of anxiety, worries or troubles; the day to day challenges we have. These have to be lifted in order to get to a place of stillness and peace. This only comes with practice. The quiet is deep enough that you can hear whispers of the inner self-voice that is in each of us. It is like soaking the dirt off your baseball uniform."

"Oh, I get it," said Joey. The dirt is like our busy thoughts and the soap and water is the meditation. So, when we are done, the clean uniform is my clear mind!"

"Once again, you amaze me, Joey, with your complete understanding."

"How often do we meditate?" asked Marissa.

"Daily practice is perfect. Start with five minutes then increase until you are at twenty minutes morning and night. Beyond that, is up to you, but that should be your goal in order to get in touch with your inner self. If you put your trust in your inner wisdom, nothing is beyond your reach."

"Can we play music during meditation, Teacher?" asked Marissa.

"I think that if it helps you, it is fine. Calm, melodic music, without words, or a guided meditation works as well. The main point is to take action and begin, to help yourself connect with your own inner wisdom."

"Teacher, so we have a breathing meditation and a pond meditation. Is there any other picture that could help us?" asked Joey.

"Yes, child. There are many images you can use. Some people like to start with an empty room, then decorate it. Others like to go to a mountain or a lake in their minds and learn from the peacefulness of nature. Let us hop on the wings of a butterfly."

"Oh cool!" exclaimed Marissa and Joey together.

"Close your eyes. Place your feet on the ground and focus on your breathing...in and out slowly. Follow your breath with your mind as you go within. Now picture a beautiful purple and blue butterfly coming down from the sky. As it comes closer, you realize that you are small enough to fit on its back so the grand wings can carry you across the land. You are quite safe and enjoy the cool breeze in your face as the butterfly takes you over green grasses and hilltops, vibrant gardens and blue waters. You notice how free you feel, without a care in the world. You are light and breezy, yet calm. You feel exuberant from the fresh air that you breathe. You have a crystal clear vision of the sky, waters and land. As you return, you bring the clarity, lightness and calm of the butterfly to your inner self."

The teacher and children sit companionably together as they follow their own breath. After a while Teacher said, "Take a deep breath and reflect on what you noticed from your journey."

"Teacher, I am so light!" exclaimed Marissa.

"And I am filled with tingles," added Joey.

"Very good children. Carry those feelings as you go throughout your day, making choices more easily, guided by calmness and peace," explained Teacher.

"I feel like I took a rest and I AM ready for my day," said Joey. "I AM within! It is the inside me that supports the me you see!"

"I see the inside me too!" agreed Marissa.

"You are so right, dear ones. I am glad that we shared this time. Let us walk in the garden, back to our homes."

So the teacher and children walked along, feeling the peace and contentment that meditation has brought them. They knew they would be ready for their day. They have a new tool, meditation, which will aid them in the daily journey of life.

CPSIA information can be obtained
at www.ICGtesting.com
Printed in the USA
397722LV00001B/1